EMOETRY:

of a fragmented human
overwhelmed with titles

EMOETRY:
of a fragmented human
overwhelmed with titles

ANITRA EVANS

LaunchCrate Publishing
Kansas City, KS

Emoetry is a work of poetry. Names, characters, places, and incidents are either the productions of the author's experience.

Emoetry
Written by Anitra Evans

© 2021 Anitra Evans

ALL RIGHTS RESERVED. No part of this publication may be reproduced, distributed, or transmitted in any form or by any means, including photocopying, recording, or other electronic or mechanical methods, without the prior written permission of the publisher, except in the case of brief quotations embodied in critical reviews and certain other noncommercial uses permitted by copyright law. For permission requests, email the publisher with subject "Attention: Permissions Coordinator," at the email address below.

LaunchCrate Publishing
Kansas City, KS
info@launchcrate.com
www.launchcrate.com

Ordering Information:
Quantity sales. Special discounts are available on quantity purchases by corporations, associations, and others. For details, contact the publisher at the email address above. Orders by U.S. trade bookstores and wholesalers.

Library of Congress Control Number: 2021908075

Hardcover ISBN: 978-1-947506-26-8

Printed in the United States of America
10 9 8 7 6 5 4 3 2 1

First Edition

INTRODUCTION

Life is never an easy journey. Everyone experiences the valleys and mountain peaks here and there; however, the thing that we remember most are the valleys. Valleys are the trials and consequences of life choices that challenge us to either become a victim or a phoenix. Now although we would all like to rise above the ashes and see the beauty from our pain, many of us don't. We become victims to our life choices and the choices of others that effect us.

It is easy to become a victim. I am not going to lie, I am still walking on the path of not being a victim. Personally, I still have victim mentality moments every now and then; especially when I encounter situations that can cause me to become frozen in my ability to take action.

Let me define victim mentality so that there is no confusion. Victim mentality causes you to become frozen in a specific time, and not allowing yourself (or being able) to work through it. This stagnation begins to trickle over into just about every area of your life, causing you to get to such a low point that you are not even surviving; but honestly waiting to die. In this wait of death, your communication with others become toxic because your view of self is toxic. Now toxic doesn't always reflect your interaction with others, but can reflect your way of living for yourself. For me, it showed itself as me being a doormat for anybody. This way of communication causes you to be placed in a box that doesn't allow for you to grow because you are continually forming yourself to others' expectations. As much as we don't want to mention or acknowledge this, this is a truth that must be faced, to start taking steps into becoming the woman who rises in beauty from ashes.

How does the fire start that causes us the damage to end up rising from ashes? Sometimes these fires that cause our ashes happen, because of our choices. For example, not listening to the advice or wisdom of others, because of pride or ignorance. It can also come from the ignorance and maliciousness of others, such as rape being your first sexual encounter. Or, sometimes it is a combination of both, they come from your own and another's lack in an area, such as a first love that was steeped in scandals, lies and domestic abuse. These are all snapshots of stories from my pain that almost caused me to become a victim of choices. And from those moments in time came these writings, from a period in my life that everyone experiences, the period of pain and trials. So never think too little or too highly of your pain, just see it for the moment

Introduction

that it is, asking the Most High for understanding of how this belongs in the novel of your life.

Now, to the root of why this book was created. I have had a couple of traumatizing moments with men. But the most trauma I ever endured was with the father of my daughters. This book encompasses writings from two very distinctive and traumatic time periods that I experienced with him. The inspirational devotional comes out of our first round of rendezvous from 2014 to 2016.

After our first 2 years, I was in a broken place of mental shock from the damage he had done. I shared the word of Yahuah with other women, as a hope to rebuild myself after what I thought was love lost; while encouraging women around me, who I knew (or thought) could use the encouragement. The best way to fill up, is to pour out. From there I gained strength, but my love and want of being a family with the father of my daughter led me back to him.

The second round of writings which includes the emoetry and short stories that bubbled out of me, came after the final blows of all that he had done to break me, and the blows I had dealt to myself because I thought and didn't listen when advice was given to me about him. The second timeframe had me lost in the worst way, where I had hit the valley of death. And not because he didn't want me, but because I had let myself get to that point of dejection, by becoming the nightmare I had always promised to never be; a single mother of multiple children, getting government assistance. From that place I had to choose to live or die, not only for me, but for the 2 young girls I was about to embark on raising. I took as much of the anguish and all of the emotions that I could process, and I began to write.

That is why I wrote this book; as a way for women to begin their process of rising from the ashes of any situation that they may have been put in. With your own stories, no one can tell you how traumatic they are and if you deserve to be a victim or not. If you find yourself in the mentality above after a situation, only you can initiate the process to become a finished work.

DAY 1

Proverbs (Mishlei) 31:10

"Who can find a virtuous woman? for her price is far above rubies."

Day 1

What is your worth? How does Yahuah view you? How do you view yourself? How do others view you? Do you and others view you how Yahuah views you? These are the questions that I have had to ask myself recently, because I was beginning to realize that my communication with myself and the world around me weren't on the same level. I felt as if I wasn't being heard, and as if what I had to say was irrelevant. I then began to feel irrelevant, which was beginning to have an effect on my self-view. I was spiraling and then I just realized, this had to stop. I have had my share of self-esteem issues throughout life, but this point was the bottom. That is when this scripture entered into my life, and I begin to realize, how I see myself, is not the same way that my Creator sees me.

You can't let the views of this world or even of yourself begin to destroy the beautiful jewel that Yahuah has made you to be. So with that being said, to get a jewel, someone has to search and dig to get to it. Allow, no better yet, make people search to receive you. Just like Yahusha Ha'Mashiach did when He was flesh and walked the earth. He spoke in ways that many times angered and or confused the people who he was talking to. That whole process, was Yahusha Ha'Mashiach taking the time to have people search for His value, which was given to him by our Creator. But what is so crazy is, when Yahusha Ha'Mashiach died and rose, his value multiplied so much that his worth overflowed.

The result, ultimately gives you your value, which is priceless. So now again I ask you, what is your worth?

Greetings. If you are reading this, it is because Yah has your heart in mind. We are all women wanting to be the best that we can be, no matter the walk. Whether you are a student, career woman, mother or wife (which as a woman many of us are all plus more.); either way, no matter which hat we wear, we cannot expect to do all of this by ourselves. We need help. Whether it is from those around us, or those silent moments of tears with Yah, that lead us to a peace and strength like nothing we have ever had before. Each day for the next 21 days, you will read a scripture that captures a righteous characteristic and the essence of the ultimate woman. I am on a journey to find out who is the woman that Yah has created me to be, and how do I get there?

Come take this journey with me, so that in this year and the years to come, we can be the most successful women that we are meant to be. Even in wearing the many hats that make us up; so that we can learn to embrace the intersectionality of our life and not compartmentalize our life.

Readers Disclaimer: Read each day and ask Yah to give you eyes to see and ears to hear.

Day 2

Proverbs (Mishlei) 31:11-12

11 "The heart of her man safely trusts in her, so that he shall have no need of spoil.

12 "She will do him good and not evil all the days of her life."

"HER HUSBAND DEPENDS ON HER. HE WILL NEVER BE POOR. SHE DOES GOOD FOR HER HUSBAND ALL HER LIFE. SHE WILL NEVER CAUSE HIM TROUBLE." (ERV)

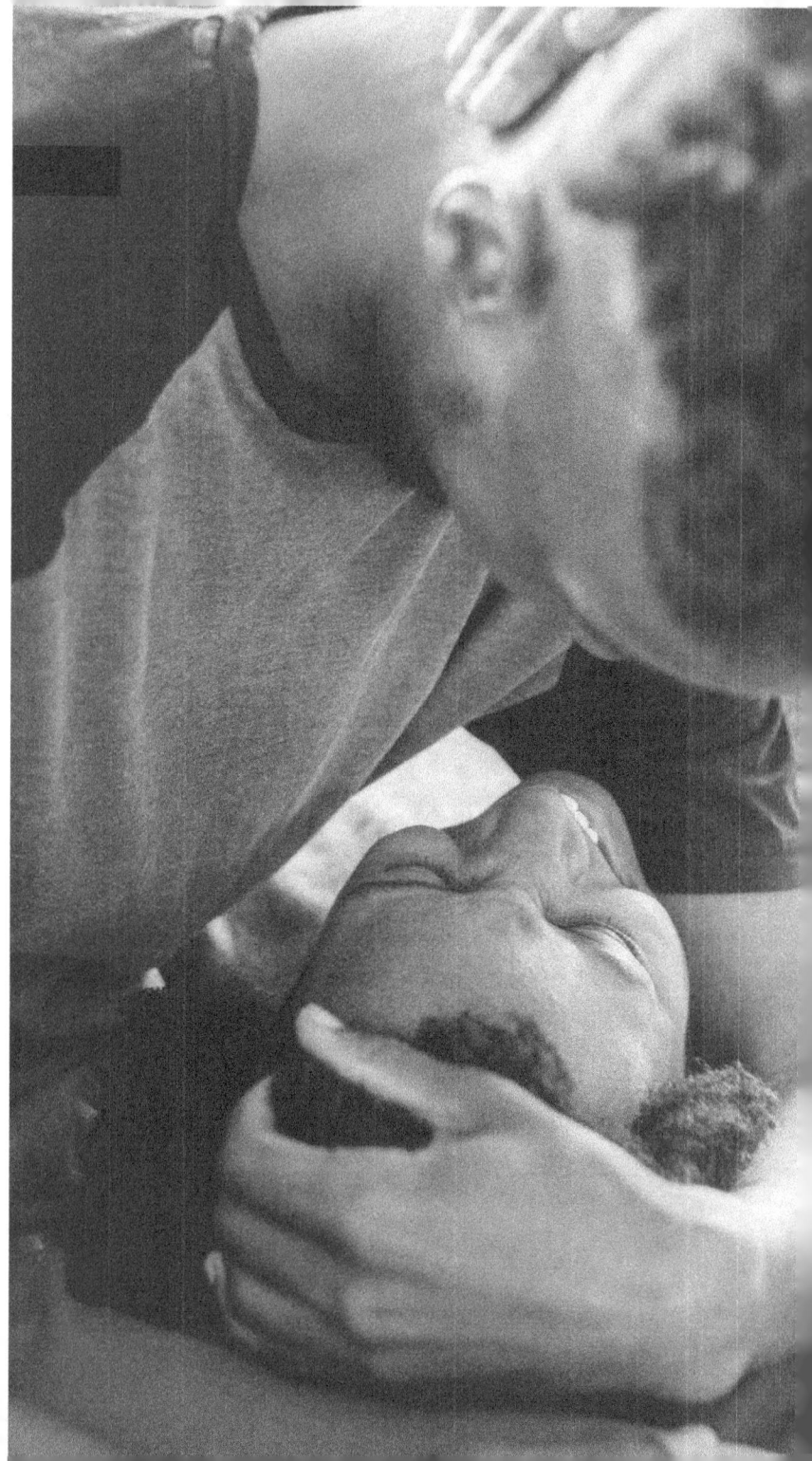

Day 2

I listed this scripture in two ways, because we all have our own opinions and perspective on life, especially concerning men and our relationship with them. Now, I'm not going to give some preachy break down of this scripture. Read it and ask Yahuah what it means for you at this time. It can have a completely different meaning for a single woman with no kids, compared to a married woman with kids, and all of those in between. Just take this one thing into account, no matter where you are in terms of relationships:

AT ALL TIMES, treat yourself with the RESPECT and DIGNITY that you expect your mate (and honestly the rest of the world) to treat you with. (Refer back to day one and knowing your worth.) Make sure you are faithful to yourself and most importantly your relationship with Yahuah as the lover of your soul (literally).

Hopeless? Hope?

My mind is racing oh so fast.
No medicine for this addiction,
How long will it last?
It's a mental, emotional and physical disease.

Everyone has their opinions and advice, but no one takes time to see the device that is holding me down, pound for pound. I try to move forward but I'm stuck like a hound.

Guarding a well-kept secret that is starting to take me down. Everyone blames him, but it started before. He was just the piece of hay that finally made me crash through the floor. So now I'm here fighting for my life, so that my kids don't know pain and they don't know strife. But the fight gets harder each and every day. Maybe I was too weak for this world, so I'm getting less motivated to stay.

All the things I wanted were simple. And now I see, how real the devil is, because he finally

Day 2

got me. he has me in the box that he always wanted me in. Started years ago with no type of defense. People played with me and became my enemy, used my love for Yah against me to spread their idiocies. So now I'm left to pick up the pieces, so hurt and damaged that I can't even see them. So instead of doing the work, part of me just wants to die. But the greater part in me says you have to strive. Going for the goal ahead, although I can't see it. Each day wondering oh why can't I beat it? Where am I going ? What is there? But yet I continue walking, knowing that it is fair. Something wild beyond my dreams if I just could hold on. Fingers slipping off the cliff, that I never knew that I was on. Praying not to fall while expecting the inevitable.

What happens if I fall and He catches me, the incomparable.

7/17/2017

Day 3

Proverbs (Mishlei) 31:13-14

13 "She seeks wool, and flax, and works willingly with her hands. 14 She is like the merchants' ships; she brings her food from afar."

Day 3

Don't limit yourself! Through Yahuah, get all of the resources that you need to have a stable home, and function in all of the gifts, skills and talents which you have obtained throughout life. As you gain wisdom, it can be applied to the areas above to exercise in the proper balance of your interaction of family and outside world.

Also, allow for many channels to be your income, not just one "planned" job or career. Most of the time to do this, you have to step out of your comfort zone to achieve these things. Don't limit yourself, because Yahuah has given you many visions to achieve in this life. Only you can decide to follow His vision for you.

Hope you all had a blessed day and if it didn't turn out like you wanted, know that your tomorrow doesn't have to reflect today. Turn back to the path of wisdom that guides your spirit in truth.

_____

I love you

Many times the closest People will use their, "I love you," as a welcome mat to smear and wipe all of their dirt on to you. Calling it advice and opinion, only clogs up your mental and emotional space with more of the dirt and germs wiped in your face (space).

Time and time again, you welcome them back in. Wondering what you should do with the stained mat at the entrance. You let them sit, at times wine and dine, allowing them storage within your state of mind. All of the while, the mat is getting dirtier and dirtier, amidst of the junk that they carry wherever they go.

With each visit you begin to say please leave some of your junk at the door (as you point in the way.) The conversations become less and the atmosphere more restricted. Finally the day comes, they decide not to sit in. Only instead to wipe their feet once more. And there

Day 3

remains the mat of the forgotten love at the door.

Stung with a choice to wash it or throw it away. You look at the mat and decide it's time to...

7/27/2017

Day 4

Proverbs (Mishlei) 31:15

15 "She rises also while it is yet night,
and gives meat to her household,
and a portion to her maidens."

Day 4

Ladies,

Make sure that those around you are well taken care of. This does not always mean money. The first way you can care for your family, is making sure that they know who Yahuah is and how to live according to His Torah. Through that wisdom and understanding, they know that as easily as they can talk to you, they can talk to HIM. For we don't live only on bread, but by every word that comes from Yahuah (Gospel of Luke- Besorah Luqas 4:4 and Deuteronomy- Devariym 8:3).

Now, back to the physical world we live in. Provide for your family always! Those in your house, your husband, children and their children should be cared for mentally, physically and spiritually. You are the support for the keeper of the gate and the inhabitants. Next comes that of the community that is around you. We all have different people and relationships in our lives. So first, you have to be sure that you are in a mental and emotional safe place to be able to be a happy helper to the community around you. Whether it's a roommate, friend or literally a maid; look out and assist those who are surrounding you with compassion and a helping hand.

Emoetry

DON'T EVER FEEL COMPELLED TO ASSIST OR CARE FOR AN ENEMY. DON'T DO HARM TO THEM, BUT ALSO KNOW YOU DO NOT HAVE TO HAVE THEM IN YOUR SPACE.

Day 4

MY NIGHTMARE. MY DREAM.

I took the time, I took the chance. Left me with two kids to do the single mother dance. My worst nightmares are coming true, a creative woman stuck in the corporate world with no savior. Working every day and night for the man's dreams without a fight... And finally when I'm off his clock. Left to go home to a bunch of socks. Thrown about the room, raising 2 kids alone. That 35000 I make barely makes a home. I feel like I might as well be working at McDonald's making nickels and pennies with no one to spot 'em.

I guess if I listened to what everyone was saying, I wouldn't be here contemplating. But I listened to my heart, with no regret. Only wishing that he could see that he had the best yet.

7/27/2017

Day 5

Proverbs (Mishlei) 31:16

16 "She considers a field, and buys it: with the fruit of her hands she plants a vineyard."

Day 5

You probably thought this was a Monday through Friday job...well, NAW! The devil never sleeps in attacking us, so I am not sleeping in my work.

Now this scripture really has me, because it is talking about the biggest struggle we all have... finances. There, I said it, we have identified the money sucking elephant in the room and our life. Now what can we do to be better? On Day 4, I said 'make sure those around you are well taken care of. This may not always be money.' So with that, we can gain an understanding of what is being stated: use your resources to make sure that you are doing your part to keep your family cared for, (whether that is children from your loins or just friends that are as close to you as a sister).

We do still live in a world where money is a big factor. So with this scripture, I feel as if Yahuah is saying be WISE with your spending. Before you make any purchase (not including purchases for your basic necessities), really think and visualize how useful this purchase will be in your life. How long will it last? Will it benefit my family, or even myself? If yes then buy it. But always think before you buy, and don't buy on impulse.

As a new mother, that has been my biggest problem...impulse buying. See my problem is, I want my baby to have everything. But I have to realize that the way my bank account is setup, I have to consider things before just buying. Sometimes, we think something is important at the time; and upon paying, we realize that maybe Yah wasn't trying to lead us in that way. So with any purchase, use it as a learning lesson; not condemning yourself as you learn financial literacy.

The next part is dear to my heart. Once, a long time ago, men were in charge of finances in the family. However, in this lifetime, we see more and more women taking over the role of financial provider. So whether as a woman who has assumed the role of financier for the house or just contributing, know that the labor of your hands does not go unnoticed by Yahuah. And, as you work diligently, you will reap what you sow. Just keep the faith (also known as hope) in Yahuah and His role as our provider. He will provide for you through the work that you are doing, as well as what you are not doing. Do not stop the work, even when people do not give you the praise you deserve; because everything is done unto Yahuah.

Day 5

LIVING IN A MILLENNIAL WORLD

Living in a millennial world there's two ways to go.

You can go up or you can stay frozen. It seems like there are only two types when looking at our actions.

The ones shining and dining, working and refining, making and shaking, moving and baking. Pictures on the gram, status in the book, Snapchat filter always ready to look. Faces smiling, just enough friends, money long enough to make amends. Parents are proud and if not they still living life without giving them thought.

Then there are the others, frozen in time. Trying to walk forward but each step seems to lead them behind. Wanting to cross the burning sands, but directed by a **voice** from

deep within. That whispers so surely keep your peace. People say they know **me** but have not seen. You understand as others shun;
the life I lived wasn't full of fun, stacks or even bubble gum simplicity.

Striving daily to listen within, opening my mind to change my sin...nature and teachings from this world below. Everything I get comes from my Elohim fo sho. So frozen millennial, don't give in to doubt, but continue to live another day. Learning and growing on the inside, because believe me one day, you will fly. (that your fruit will bear on the outside.)

12/10/2017

Day 6

Proverbs (Mishlei) 31:17

17 "She girds her loins with strength, and strengthens her arms."

SELF CARE ISN'T SELFISH

Day 6

This scripture says it all in terms of the body: make sure your body is cared for. Now, self-care doesn't equal you being some super gym/diet guru, looking as close to a Kardashian as possible. It does mean that you have to care for your body in the state that you are in, and this has been a big battle of mine for like, all (of) my life. I have always been on the heavy side physically, and I hated my body. So that caused me to begin yo-yoing with my body and health. At points in life, I can be physically fit for my body type, and other times I can be obese. No matter where I am in either point of my life, my goal was always to look a certain way based on society's perspective. But after looking deeper into this scripture, and really trying to understand my worth through Yahuah (and how he should reflect through me), I realized that Yahuah just wants us all to be healthy and physically in a place where we are able to keep up with the demands of life, and not be physically exhausted all of the time.

So ladies, begin to change your thinking to know that you are fearfully and wonderfully made (Psalm {Tehilliym} 139:14) by Yahuah, and that He loves you the way that you are. (I mean He did create you!) No matter what people on this earth may say, you must stand on the word of Yahuah when seeing your beauty. Change your eyes to see yourself the way Yah sees you! Now…just because you love yourself, does not mean let yourself go. Make sure you keep your body fit, not just for you but for your family and the destiny that Yahuah has for you.

Day 6

THOUGHTS

At first the thought of your leaving was way beyond me. I felt like it was a nightmare that you kept romanticizing as a dream.

I fought and I fought because the thought of being without you felt like a life that I couldn't do. I couldn't walk on my own because you gave me everything. I couldn't talk on my own because your words were my being.

And then just like that, like all of those years didn't matter, you took your being away just to leave me flatter. Low to the ground, trying to find a way up, but all I get is a hole that you left me stuck.

It's funny how the people that should care for you the most, put the most damage in your life.

But you must continue to look up. I promise to be nothing like you, because as a parent, you know what you do. And it's okay because

Emoetry

you tried to let money and status raise me.
But because I know of better, I will spread my
wings and fly. Never die, never limited to your
fantasy and lie. And all of this as an example,
so that my girls will never have to worry for
being on my back. So the day that they too
can finally soar, I'll be flying right below them
raising them up more and more.

10/15/2017

Day 7

Proverbs (Mishlei) 31:18-19

18 "She perceives that her merchandise is good: her candle goes not out by night.

19 She lays her hands to the spindle, and her hands hold the distaff."

Day 7

Now today started off as one of those "ughhh… it's Monday" kind of days. Everything in me wanted to give up before even trying. I mean hey, we have days like that. I then began to study the next round of scriptures of our reading, and realized that I did not understand a thing it was saying. So I became frustrated and the day went on (as so). All day I tried to send this encouragement out, but my frustration was hindering me from allowing myself to open up and allow for my spirit to gain an understanding of the scriptures.

So after sitting down and realizing that some of my frustration was coming from not understanding some of the words in the scripture and its usage (side note: most of the time, our frustration comes from a lack of understanding the situation or the people around us.), I then sat down and looked up perceiveth and distaff online. After finding the meaning and some explanations of the historical context of this type of woman's work, and putting this scripture into lingo that I could understand, I realized what Yahuah was saying through this scripture.

He was saying know the worth of the work that you do with your hands, and never stop. Don't stop because someone tells you to stop, or even bigger, because you tell yourself to stop (the self is our biggest enemy, until we train it to be our biggest supporter). Another facet on top of knowing the value of your product or skill, is the continuing journey of seeking knowledge and understanding, in your career/job, skill set and or hobby. Never limit yourself because Yah has not limited you. Never give up on yourself, because Yahusha Ha'Mashiach has not given up on you. And as your sister, I want you to know that I am in your corner and I haven't given up on you or limited you either.

Day 7

Learning.Of.Violent.Encounters

My love for you goes on and on, many times I want to pick up the phone. To call, text or just look at your face. To remember the good times of our solid place.

But the emotions start to flood back. Jealousy, insecurity, the feeling of being stabbed in the back, through my heart.

A rough start, placing the memories of the time we spent together. In those moments lost in you, not knowing that most of it wasn't true. Saying you're finessing each and every girl. But the only one being finessed is the one who gave up her world for you. And all you can do is throw it back in her face and say shame on you.

Always threats of replace and knives in my face. Guilt and shame I carry of being a victim of the month of October, the ribbon that's purple. Can add that to the list of things that I wouldn't wish on anyone today or tomorrow.

I keep my mouth closed because I don't want to stain your name more than is already thought. But I can't keep going back for the strength of my daughters and I, because I never want them to grow up thinking it's okay for a man to manipulate you and threaten you every other day.

Not saying there wasn't times of love. Which is probably why I hold on so strong. But I prefer to live and watch my girls grow. I don't want to die because of your nature to control.

10/17/2017

Day 8

Proverbs (Mishlei) 31:20

20"She stretches out her hand to the poor; yea, she reaches forth her hands to the needy."

Day 8

GIVE!!!! When you have, give.

That (once again) doesn't mean money; but it means taking the time to meet someone where they are with a need. This can include, but not limited to, giving food, a necessity, a kind word or even a hug.

Give without expecting anything in return.

"GIVE, AND IT WILL BE GIVEN TO YOU. THEY WILL POUR INTO YOUR LAP A GOOD MEASURE-PRESSED DOWN, SHAKEN TOGETHER, AND RUNNING OVER [WITH NO SPACE LEFT FOR MORE]. FOR WITH THE STANDARD OF MEASUREMENT YOU USE [WHEN YOU DO GOOD TO OTHERS] IT WILL BE MEASURED TO YOU IN RETURN." (Luke {Besorah Luqas} 6:38).

Another side note: Giving with the expectation of a return is called a loan. THAT IS NOT FREELY GIVING. Just so no one is confused.

ASMADE

When will enough be enough? All the pain and suffering you take just for his sake.

Many nights alone no call or response on the phone.

Lies of sitting and working but evidence goes against ya.

Sipping and laughing, enjoying time with ya chickens(b******).

Talking about they mean nothing, still more lies. Because if you was true like me, they wouldn't even catch your eye.

But I guess I'll be the fool continuously until I take the time to set me free.

Free of the love that I have for you. The love that created two wonderful jewels. Jewels that for you were too hard to find, because to you

Day 8

they weren't people, they were just apart of mine.

My(mine) being, and none of you. The only time they received love, was when I got your love too. Other than that for you we were a package, of good old memories and future baggage.

10/17/2017

Day 9

Proverbs (Mishlei) 31:21-22 (KJV)

21 "She is not afraid of the snow for her household: for all her household are clothed with scarlet.

22 "She makes herself coverings of tapestry; her clothing is silk and purple."

Day 9

This scripture is pretty straight forward. Clothes, attire, fashion, so on and so forth, we must keep ourselves and our family clothed. Not just in anything, but as the old folks say, "with common sense." We must dress daily in a way that keeps us modest and whole where ever we go.

The colors and material used in this scripture refers to the attire that was worn by royalty and those of a higher class. So in all that you do, carry yourself with dignity and know that you are royalty, because you are a child of THE ONLY TRUE KING, as long as YOU serve HIM.

Do not be afraid of the things on this earth, because we are in the Ha'Masiach, and in Him we are renewed into the life that Yahuah originally had for us. Through Yahuah, we are whole and we have EVERYTHING that we need. So, I want to take today as a day to remind us that we are royalty, and to thank Yahuah for bestowing such a wonderful gift on us. And if you don't know Yahuah as your Ha'Masiach, the one who has given you life through His TORAH, take the time to learn Him and thank Him for giving you complete freedom to not have to endure the curses of life that were originally set for and before you.

Thank Him and take time to enjoy the abundance of Yah's grace, His presence and His promises for your life by "putting on" TORAH as your mental garment.

Love you all.

Day 9

In to me see

Once upon a time the thought of intimacy with you, was the air that I breathed and the thought that I pursued. Not sex, but the conversation, drives along the highway and songs in rotation. Parking lot sessions just you me and the beat, oh and can't forget the baby in the backseat. Sleeping away in love that created her, knowing that the guardians of her galaxy were always in play.

Our love was like fireworks blazing in the sky. I couldn't wait to connect to you and create an electricity so true. That it would shock the hell out of us and renew. But you know what they say when lightning strikes 3 times. The negative energy begins to vibe.

From dusk til dawn I waited for you. But then dusk just became night, and I was afraid of you. The same energy that I used to run to you, is the same I now use to mentally get over you.

Your first love they say. Is why it hurts so bad. But the pain isn't from the love, it's from the betrayal and lies. The way I use to crave for your in to me see(intimacy). I now wish it was all just a vivid dream. I try to close my eyes and dream of being close to you, now all I see is the death in my truth. I couldn't kiss you or lay with you or even talk to you. A stain on my wedding dress is how I now view you. What was once pure and only meant for a special occasion, you have trampled on and caused destruction for no known reason.

I guess it just means your season has passed.

The only thing that makes all of this hard to swallow, is because although right now you don't want to be in the girls life, you can come back whenever you want. Just don't try to cause strife.

11/2/2017

Day 10

Proverbs (Mishlei) 31:25

25 "Strength and honour are her clothing; and she shall rejoice in time to come."

Day 10

To wear strength and honor at all times is something that really comes in handy on the days it seems as if everything is against you. It is easy to possess these articles when things are good or even okay. But, what about when tribulation comes and people are speaking bad about you, or you have to make decisions that seems so hard to bare?

Remember to dress in the armor of Yah, and allow His word to be your shield (Ephesians {Eph'siym} 6:14-17). This means allow for your inner woman (spirit) to be dressed with the word of Yah, so that it builds your faith and character as a woman. Then allow for that inner coat to permeate your outer woman (physical manifestations), thus clothing you with the strength that comes in your joy from Yah and the honor of being part of the court of the King of kings and the Elohim of elohiym . Here are some scriptures to clothe you in strength and honor:

"REJOICE IN HOPE; BE PATIENT IN TRIBULATION; AND ALWAYS PRAYING." (ROMANS {Romaiym} 12:12)

THERE HAS NO TEMPTATION TAKEN YOU, BUT SUCH AS IS COMMON TO MAN: BUT YAHUAH IS

FAITHFUL, WHO WILL NOT SUFFER YOU TO BE TEMPTED ABOVE THAT YE ARE ABLE; BUT WILL WITH THE TEMPTATION ALSO MAKE A WAY TO ESCAPE, THAT YE MAY BE ALE TO BEAR IT. (1 CORINTHIANS {Qorintiym Ri'shon} 10:13)

Do not give up in the midst of the hardest battle. But stand in the strength of the Elohim and the honor of His word to "NEVER LEAVE YOU OR FORSAKE YOU." (DEUTERONOMY {Devariym} 31:6)

He had never really been physical much before. To say a cheater: yes, not appreciative of me: yes; but never had he put his hands on me before. So the first time that this occurred. It had put me in a stand-still and shock. I didn't understand how someone who stated that they love me so much; could find it in them to put their hands on me.

The first time that I recall was in January

Day 10

2017. We had just moved into our new apartment together to start a new life. It was myself, our sweet daughter, a roommate and him. Not really knowing what would occur, we moved in hopes of being able to be a family that we always dreamed of and talked about. Not realizing that all of the brokenness of our childhood would come to a boiling point.

One evening, I don't really recall how we got there, but we had been arguing. Most of the time, it was always my fault, because working a 10 hr shift four to five days a week and then ubering afterwards; he would clock my time. And if the time frames didn't make sense, then of course I was doing something that I wasn't supposed to be doing. I was either cheating or being mischievous by his accounts. With that being said, I can't recall what had caused the fight this night, but he had been taking part of his daily ritual of drinking and smoking. And he was upset, and I didn't want it to get as bad as it had before with the screaming, so I said, "I am going to leave." Not that I was leaving for good, it was more of an I am stepping out so that you can calm down. I don't want this atmosphere around our daughter. Well that was an ignition to a side of his anger that I had never seen before.

I began to feel myself being pushed down to the ground; repeatedly feeling his hands pushing me back and down at the same time.

Coming from the family of women that I come from, abuse has never been a situation that we have encountered. SO, my mentality was I am not going to let you put your hands on me and think you are going to get away with it. So I began to kick at him. I kicked him back and I tried to fend him off. I swung my fist and I hit him one good time across his cheek. And in my mind, I thought, "good...this will get him to stop." However, it had an opposite effect.

Day 10

His eyes became more bulging and red, and it was like it lit a fire in him. It was a green light for him to say, "now I can put my hands on you like a man." I can't remember much, but I remember him pushing me into the closet and punching my face repeatedly and scratching at me. At this point I was just trying to protect myself and get away; as my little daughter was just standing there. I screamed out for my roommate and asked her to just grab my baby so that she wouldn't get hurt and/or see what was happening to Mommy. She scooped my daughter up and took her to the room. As he continued to wail on me, he just suddenly stopped and looked at me; and he said, "don't ever leave me." And with that he turned around and walked away and left the house.

I was scared, not going to lie; but I wasn't scared enough to leave. I was afraid of this abuse becoming a cycle, and my daughter growing up seeing that. With that, I realized, that going forward, I had to change my approach when dealing with him. I decided to lay down.

Day 11

Proverbs (Mishlei) 31:26

26 "She opens her mouth with wisdom; and in her tongue is the Torah of kindness."

Day 11

Keeping it simple. When being wise with your response, you should be sure to listen, ready to learn and not just to talk back (James {Ya'aqov} 1:19). When you really listen, it can allow for you to respond out of wisdom and not the first thing that pops into your head or mouth. You must also be wise to know when to respond with words and when not to respond with words. Everything in the world doesn't need a verbal response, many times an action can speak louder than any amount of words you'll ever say.

We all have heard the saying, "If you don't have nothing nice to say, don't say it all." So, when you speak to people, you don't always have to be soft and say "good things" within your conversation. But, when you do speak to people, you should be sure to speak to them in a tone of respect that you would want to receive from others. Don't allow your emotions to get the best of your verbal response.

Another side to a tongue of kindness, is not allowing for your words to hinder people, whether that is with continuous false praise or continuous criticism. Speak life into people, not death.

Poem 9

A dream deferred is the equivalent to feeling like a turd.

Missed out opportunities, knowing in your heart and soul that there is so much more, intricacies of life that you skipped so you try and recover (remember).

The base of your dream or heart's desire, so that the soul can release on the earth your awesome fire. Works undone and unknown, searching to achieve your glorious crown given by the one.

11/13/2017

Day 12

Proverbs (Mishlei) 31:27

27 "She looks well to the ways of her household, and eats not the bread of idleness."

Day 12

Do not be lazy! Never stop growing or advancing! Not being idle does not mean keeping yourself busy with just anything. Just because you are doing something, does not mean you are growing. Idleness is not gauged by how much action you do, but by how much growing you do. Don't be idle and stagnate in your growth spiritually, mentally, emotionally, physically and any other -ly you can think of.

With that being said, we as women can sometimes over work ourselves with the demands that life throws at us, and those we take on. Now, what I am about to say will cause some of you to flip. However, once you come back down to earth, reflect and think about how true this is to your life.

IT IS OKAY TO REST.

There, I said it. As you are growing in life, and bobbing and weaving through its demands, balance yourself with rest. Resting is not being lazy, it is the opportunity to replenish yourself from all that you have poured out into the world. It is you being filled up, so you can finish the tasks at hand. Think of it like this, a glass of ice cold water has the duty of quenching the thirst of the person who is demanding that it purpose be fulfilled. However, if the person drinks all of the water, the glass no longer has any use; UNLESS it is replenished with more ice cold water. You are the glass, the ice cold water is what you have to offer, and the person is of course the demands of life. Do not allow yourself to die before your purpose is fulfilled, because you did not replenish yourself; spiritually, physically, or mentally/emotionally.

REMEMBER, your spirit should always be the first thing to replenish with the use of the ever flowing water of the Ha'Masiach. (John {Besorah Yahuchanon} 4:13-14 and 7:37-38)

Day 12

Pasos

I had to take the first step, before I could take any more.

Before I could walk through the open door of blessings and prosperity, I had to walk up the hall of battle and conquest.

Deep breaths of frustration. Hopes lost to temptation. All of the scenarios running in my head as I lay with two kids in the bed.

Both pushed from the essence of my strife. Swam in the bosom of my milk to retain life.

Given to me as hope and freedom and a reason to press on.

To walk along that long path not cutting through the grass.

To make it to the door and walk through not for less but more.

11/20/2017

Day 13

Proverbs (Mishlei) 31:29-30

29 "Many daughters have done virtuously, but you excel them all.

30 Favour is deceitful, and beauty is vain: but a woman that fears YAHUAH, she shall be praised."

Day 13

Many things from this scripture stand out, but our focus on this day is TO FEAR YAHUAH! And no, I am not talking about the fear that causes you to be scared of Yah to the point that it blocks your relationship with Him. The "fear" that Yah is conveying to us as His children, is one that comes from love and respect. This kind of "fear" could be exemplified by a child who even in fear of the choices they have made, which have yielded negative consequences, still tells their parents. They tell their parents because they know that their parents will still love them. And as a parent (although the child may not always understand) will allow for the consequences to come, they remain there as a support beam for the child. This is Yah to us, a loving parent who will move heaven and earth for us to see and experience this love.

He is not out to get us. But, because there are consequences for our actions based on the way the world works, He is there all of the time supporting us and carrying us through the storm - even if we don't see or know it. Now quick side note, this is reflective of a parent and child relationship. Everyone is not a child of Yahuah, so in that case, the above mentioned support does not apply to them. Now let us continue.

If you have children or at some point in life you have been a child, you can surely relate to the want of an open line of communication. We as people just want to have someone who we can talk to and get answers from. Parents who love us in words and actions, as we mature in what we say or do; knowing that we will always need them but allowing us to make choices based on the instruction that they instilled in us. This is Yah. He wants to give us this perfect relationship and love (thanks to the instructions He has given us, and the release from curses through Yahusha TORAH). So "fear Yahuah", with no hindrance, just love.

Day 13

I remember

I remember sitting in the hospital with my 3 week old baby.

Doctors looking and talking to me like I'm crazy,

like they know what's best for my child,
just because they went to school,
but when I ask a question they drone on like fools.

Haven't you heard of the Tuskegee test or how about the culture cells of Henrietta Lacks. So as you see with this post racial society, most of the nurses checking my daughter's IV and doctors with diagnosis; voted for the current uneducated man making proceeds to his businesses. Not caring about the little brown child and her mother who is sitting alone wondering. Praying and deliberating. She asks Yah to come and save her child. But no you prefer to try and scare her, give her the worse possibilities although the reality shows it false. Or run up a bill in further hopes to put her in financial ruin.

Either way all this doesn't matter because the truth I know, that the power of your lies will soon have to go.

11/20/2017

Day 14

Proverbs (Mishlei) 31:31

31 "Give her of the fruit of her hands: and let her own works praise her in the gates."

Day 14

Let your actions speak for you in public, not your words. Your words should only back up what you are bringing or already have brought to the table (of life). In today's world where everyone is doing more speaking (talking) than action. Be the change and show the world what a woman shining in the light of the Ha'Masiach looks like.

14"Ye are the light of the world. A city that is set on a hill cannot be hid. 15 Neither do men light a candle, and put it under a bushel, but on a menorah; and it gives light unto all that are in the house. 16 Let your light so shine before men, that they may see your good works, and glorify your Father which is in heaven." (Matthew {Besorah Mattithyahu} 5:14-16)

Everything that you do, must be done in love; from the motive of the heart, or it is just a good work done (1 Corinthians {Qorintiym Ri'shon} 13:3). And with all things that you do, you must do with the heart and the expectation to give glory to Yahuah only.

The sad truth

It pains me to say as I watch her each day. Having to go from 2 to 12 in a matter of moments. I say it's because she's intellectually advanced and her social skills are par to none, but no it's because it's the black girl way.

It's the reason why white folks see little black girls as older by the age of five. No longer the little sweet baby that they all cooed at. Now she is treated like an adult without syntax.

How can this be when she is only 2, everyone in the black community expecting the world out of you. Her white counterparts aren't dealing with this. She's walking and running and most of them can barely stand. She speaks, and white people say oh she speaks so well for her age. While black people snide and say she needs a higher guide.

Just learning to move and the world already

Day 14

on her shoulders. No wonder black women always seem so much older, yet look so much younger due to all the pent up youth. Never able to truly conceptually understand that the world wasn't meant for your shoulders, only for your hands.

11/20/2017

Day 15

Proverbs (Mishlei) 31:20

20 "He that walks with wise men shall be wise: but a companion of fools shall be destroyed."

Day 15

We are now moving into different scriptures that are not based in Proverbs 31; but are good for knowledge (or better yet wisdom) for growing in life.

I received this verse because I was watching a YouTube video of a pastor who was speaking about the importance of the company that you keep. He broke it up into three basic type of relationships that are in our life:

Divine connection - people placed in our life by Yah who remain with us for the entire journey from the point that they enter,

Divine disconnection - people who should not be in our life at all, or people we need to let go of, because their time in our life has come to an end, and

Divine reconnections - people who come back into our life, because with the first round of meeting, one or both of the parties were not ready or it wasn't time for the connection to blossom.

Understanding the breakdown of each relationship status is something very important that we as people, especially women, need to understand. So often, we as ladies allow for many people to travel in and out of our lives, taking and depositing whatever they see fit for their life. However, it is paramount for us to know who we should allow to experience this journey of life with us, who we should leave at the next stop (or on the side of the road) and who we should open a roundtrip to. For this knowledge, YOU must ask Yah daily that He connects you with the people He has ordained for your life and purpose; and that He gives you the strength to let go of those who are not conducive for your life and purpose.

Remember: **Birds of a feather flock together, but Eagles soar.** And we [ladies] want to soar in what Yah has for us.

Day 15

See you (#FACTS)

I'd like to say that I see you as the liar that you are.
A manipulating scoundrel going around stealing
hearts, like they're cars.
Joy riding on the love given to you by so many
countless souls. Using your words as the key to
open up the hearts of many; to sex, steal and finally
kill any hopes they had of being your one. But that's
not what I see.
I'd like to say that I see you as a thief in the
night. Going around to that special girl when it's
conveniently right. Quietly slipping into her domain
of peace; and snatching whatever you can take to
create this weeks feast. Singing sweet lullabies, all
the while sucking the poor girl dry, on top of all of
your lies. But that's not what I see.
I wish that I could warn all the women in the world,
but his works are so quick that you'll rarely catch

Emoetry

his licks. Here are his signs if he is near;

Bad mouth the last girl you seen him with.

Kissing and telling you it's only you he's smitten with.

Use you up and throw you away. Then he's on the run, back to his games that he play.

11/20/2017

Day 16

Romans (Romaiym) 12:12*

12 "Rejoicing in hope; patient I tribulation; continuing instant in prayer;"

*Read all of Romans 12 for a good meditation of qualities to have as a woman. But this scripture is a do all.

Day 16

Now ladies, what I am about to reveal to you is not something that is new; however, it is something that once you get a hold of what it truly means, it will change your point of view and outcome of life forever.

Tonight I was watching the movie WAR ROOM for the first time. If you have not yet seen it you MUST do so with an open heart to allow Yah to tell you about yourself. NOT EVERYONE ELSE. The main character of the movie is a married woman and a mother, who goes through a spiritual transformation that alters her mentality and overall character.

She starts out in discontentment with her marriage and life in general. Through the guidance of a mentor and a friend, she learns how to make prayer her weapon of warfare through the word of Yah. With prayer, she was able to change things (her mentality, relationship with Yah, her family and circumstances), because of her faith in Yah and the permission she gave to Him through her prayers to intervene and lead her life.

Yah is always fighting for us, and we have His ear. WE as women, just have to take the time to truly pray and seek Yah and His will for our life (which is found in the Torah of Yahuah). It could start for gain, but it should not stay that way. Allow for the Ha'Mashiach to really free you and make you new (I mean that is what He died and rose from the dead for.) Fight ladies, not against people who we see as enemies, but fight with your words given to Yah in faith, also known as prayer.

Day 16

Have You Ever

Have you ever had a knife held to your face and

asked if you were ready to die?

Have you ever been choked so hard that you felt

your life pass you by?

Have you ever been pushed, mushed and punched

while clutching your stomach praying that your

baby is okay?

The presence of death over your life only because

you want to stay.

Have you ever fought so hard to be with someone

Because in your heart you knew with them your

dreams would come true?

Have you ever had someone watch over you,

because of the danger and the atmosphere of things

around you?

Have you ever had someone chase you into the

night and hold you and hug you and say everything

Emoetry

will be alright?

Have you ever had someone who prayed over you, who talked and played with you?

Who cooked and loved you just the way you wanted?

So many things good and bad, that I ask, what is love?

If someone loves you can they lie and cheat and speak badly about you?

Can they rub and hug you at the same time, while trying to protect you?

Can they try to kill you and at the same time walk away.

Can they be with someone and tell you it's just a game?

Can you push out y'all kids, two times; with them always gone? Never by your side, leaving you all alone? But they constantly tell you, "I am building us a home."

Day 16

But when you call they barely pickup the phone? No well wished birthdays or holidays too, for the babies that they claim they love as they constantly disrespect you.

You would see the physical signs and say why are they still there. But if you could read and understand her heart. You would see doubt and fear.

Until finally one day she gets it and let's go. Not because finally she loved herself more, but more because she still loved that one, and realized that he wasn't really wanting her to be the one. Out of comfort and her continued loyalty, he always came back as a place of safety.

11/20/2017

Day 17

Psalm (Tehilliym) 27:14

14 "Wait on El-Yahuah: be of good courage, and he shall strengthen your heart: wait, I say, on El-Yahuah."

Day 17

To look at my life now, it is nothing of how I would have ever imagined for it to turn out. I am 28 years old and I am a single mother on shaky grounds with the father of my children, and to top it all off, I am below the poverty level. On the outside, that looks like a setup for the beginning of failure. HOWEVER, for my sanity in what Yahuah has already done, and the will that Yah has for me, and my daughters' sake; I CANNOT let this be the end or failure, because of what my circumstances may look like. So instead of falling into the oh so dubious trap of satan (Ha'Satan) of succumbing to what I see, I am instead learning how to be patient. By not letting what my right now seems like, be my forever. In learning how to be patient, and waiting on Yahuah's timing, I gain hope. Because in His timing, is the best alignment of all things concerning our life.

Now, sometimes we as humans, especially women, get waiting confused with just sitting around and letting life pass by. This is not so. Waiting is when you and I use our measure of faith given to us by Yah, while alleviating our disbelief in all areas of our life. We must hold on to His promise. The promise that because Yah wakes us up every day, this current situation will not be our demise and that greater is coming; because Yah said,

"GREATER IS THE ENDING OF A THING THAN THE BEGINNING." (Ecclesiastes {Qoheleth} 7:8)

So wherever you are in life, whether in a valley or the peak of a mountain; wait on Yahuah and strengthen yourself in the Torah of Yah. So that when you are in the valley or on the mountain peak, you can be thanking Yah for being faithful to His words and promises. While also leaning on Yahuah's word and promises to encourage yourself. BUT the only way to know these things and strengthen yourself is to read your bible, through the Hebraic lens of concrete living, not abstract. You can't know what Yah promises if you never read His promises. So be of good courage knowing that Yah and His word are true and waiting to do a great work with you and through you. Love you all.

Day 17

Iso F-Boy

I wake up early in the morning

Just to practice deadbeatery.

I'm the son of lies, that's what I call deceivery.

I hustle all day cause I can't make change.

Talk a big game, but when I throw I hit the frame.

You can find me in Atlanta because that's where

I stay. I try to go other places, but the jail is my

domain.

Watch out for me, I'm a wolf in sheep's clothing.

Slither like a snake so you know I ain't posing.

My dream is a family, but I don't know what that is.

Got kids runnin' around like my name is Shawty Lo.

I got Napoleon complex, so that's why I'll never

grow.

12/19/2017

Day 18

Proverbs (Mishlei) 15:1

1 "A soft answer turns away wrath: but grievous words stir up anger."

Day 18

We all have heard the saying: "If you don't have anything nice to say, don't say it at all." But what if that's not always so. I have come to realize with life's experiences, that it is not always what you say, but how you say it. When speaking with people, we must remember to have control over the words that we let come out of our mouth; and even more importantly how we say our words (the inflection and tonality). All of that matters to how a person perceives us. Now, I am not saying that you have to be a doormat to other's words; however, allow for your responses to be filled with the love and respect that you always want people to use with you.

Even if you are saying something that could be considered "mean/offensive," remember that the Torah of kindness is in the mouth of a woman (as stated in Proverbs {Mishlei} 31:26). Keep this law in your mind always, even when the initial response that you want to give is not along the lines of that law. Plus, be a part of the movement to stop hurting people; because hurt people, hurt people. And although we may feel pain, we are not people who are hurt but people of hope because of all the love given to us by Yahuah and our Ha'Masiach.

Pretty.Excited.To.Tell.Ya (P.E.T.T.Y.)

This will probably sound like I'm P.E.T.T.Y., but I want you to know that I read our Facebook messages like every day. I know you're thinking man, she is sadly obsessed with him. But no, it's not true! I do it for comfort and assurance too.

I know I am P.E.T.T.Y that I read them, but it's because I have moved on. It gives me a sense of accomplishment, like a great 90's R&B song.

I can't tell you why I'm P.E.T.T.Y, it's just the way I am, because what the devil used to try and kill me went back to the sender, and here I stand. So try to knock me down all that you want. But I'm P.E.T.T.Y enough, to tell you, I don't stand alone.

12/19/2017

Day 19

Luke {Besorah Luqas} 12:29-30

29 "And seek not ye what ye shall eat, or what ye shall drink, neither be ye of doubtful mind.

30 For all these things do the nations of the world seek after: and your Father knows that ye have need of these things."

Day 19

Today my mind was in a battle over things, that when I look back on now seem so small. Sometimes, we allow for worry to consume so much of our life, that we miss out on the moments that create the story of our life.

WAKE UP CALL: DO NOT allow for the things, concerns and situations of our daily life (bills, distracted relationships, other's words and actions, etc…) keep you from enjoying the moments that Yah has given you to make your path of life.

Devil Me

Devil when you see me

Never greet me.

Don't ever try and meet me.

All you did was try to defeat me,

But sorry boo, you're beneath me.

Like literally, underneath me.

My feet is where you're gonna be,

So take this time, start listenin'

Because of Yahuah, I'm glistenin'.

1/20/2018

Day 20

Psalm (Tehilliym) 9:10

10 "And they that know your name will put their trust in you, for you, YAHUAH, have not forsaken them that seek you."

Day 20

Plain and simple: You must know (truly understand, and have full confidence) that Yah is YOUR guide and provider. You have the choice to choose to believe in Him, by living according to the lifestyle that He has laid out to us through His Torah. Knowing that when you live a Torah lifestyle, the FACT that He will NEVER leave you is an absolute. Or, you can choose to let the everyday trials and systems of this world keep you cornered in a fetal position, causing you to serve the world's system as a slave, rather than live as Yahuah's servant.

Again, Yah will never leave you. Only you can decide to ignore Him, or get to know and build a relationship with Him.

If it is a fact that He will never leave you, what does it mean when I don't feel as if He is near? Well, Yah hasn't left, so you need to ask yourself: Have I put my faith in Yah's power? Do I believe that He is still and always with me even when I don't feel Him or can't see His power? After you get the answers to these questions, make sure your end result is you putting your trust of whatever is going on into the hands of Yah, into the ears of Yah, and into the heart of Yah. Wherever you put it, make sure it is in Yah.

He said, "31 Testimony"

He said, " I wish you would let me enjoy your body like I want to."

Baby boy hold on, let me stop you.

Just because you get some, doesn't mean you'll truly enjoy.

To enjoy my body you first have to open up my soul, my mind and then my body comes (cums).

I'm not here just for your pleasure or 20 mins of fun.

Oh don't get it twisted, I wouldn't mind backing it up on you.

Making you whine and moan in pleasure, but at the same time... My thotish ways are reserved and saved for a man who believes in all of me.

Not just temporary body touch, G.

So if you still don't understand, then obviously you ain't my man.

Day 20

Because the one who is for me, will respect my

Proverbs 31 testimony.

3/26/2018

Day 21

Isaiah (Yesha'Yahu) 9:6-7

6 "For unto us a child is born, unto us a Son is given: and the government shall be upon his shoulder: and his name shall be called Wonderful, Counselor, EL GIBBOR (the Mighty El), the Everlasting Father, the Prince of Peace.

7 Of the increase of HIS government and peace there shall be no end, upon the throne of David, and upon his kingdom, to order it, and to establish it with judgement and with justice from hence-forth even forever, the zeal of YAHUAH TSEVA'OTH will perform this."

Day 21

There is an old saying that the church folk say, "Keep yo' mind stayed on Yahusha." This is true. In all that you do (words, actions, decisions) keep your mind/ heart in tune with Yahuah through His Ruach and power. Choose to let Torah be the guiding light for your life.

We are all characters in the love story of Yahuah and His fallen lover (us - his people created out of covenant). By allowing Him to overtake us, it will change everything which results from our life. This overflow will affect our relationships, friendships, our finances, our worries/ cares, our wants/ desires and the list goes on.

So now that you have been poured into, take the time to pour into someone else. Don't keep the goodness of Yahuah and the wisdom you have gained over these past few days to yourself. Plant the seed to change someone else's life. Don't be a protagonist in this love story. Be a chapter that is fulfilled.

_____

Hey ladies...

I am sorry to say, but it is the end of our 21 day devotional. I hope this has been helpful, and that you have grown in your relationship with Yahuah, and in yourself as a woman. I hope and know that I will do this again later on, because I am called to encourage those around me. However for now, I would encourage you to reread this book to truly get a deeper revelation of Yahuah's destiny for you.

Yahuah's word is living and breathing, which means that you can always get something new, even from the same scripture. Allow for His word to breath life into you.

I have to say that I really enjoyed going through this devotional and growing with Yahuah. These particular words came to me in a time when, as a woman, I was confused and

Day 21

at my ends meet. I was a woman who'd just had a young baby (twice), and I was still in love with the father of my children, although he had recently married [the first time] and was causing me domestic trouble [the second time].

I needed Yah to show me how He saw me, and show me just a bit of my worth that I have through Him. While going through this, I was encouraged to share this journey with a few close friends and associates. If you truly opened yourself up during these 21 days, I know that you have gained something. And even if you didn't, keep re-reading it to get the breakthrough that Yah desires for your life.

Now to the poetry. That aspect allowed me to write through my feelings in a constructive

way. I did not want to hold on to these thoughts
so that they would be become bitterness and
resentment. To do so, I had to write out what
I felt in my heart in a way that would not
compromise the person/people who caused the
pain.

Thank you for allowing me to be part of your
experience. I am encouraged that you are
sowing into yourself and the truth of what
Yah has laid out for you and His people. We as
women are jewels. And by being the help-mate
to the men, we hold a standard not only for
ourselves or them, but for society as a whole.

About the Author

Before 2010, when I imagined life, all I could picture was my road to success. I knew it would not be an easy journey, because microaggression of others around me were nothing new to me. However, year in and year out, I continue to take in each trial and make it my triumph.

I am a mother, community activist and business owner; born and raised in Kansas City, Missouri, determined not to allow the boundaries of the Midwest keep me shackled in a mindset that stymied self-expression of the Black creative. Educated at Spelman College in Atlanta Ga, I was afforded the opportunity to live in the Dominican Republic and Spain to further my studies. In these places, I begin to see and speak to women of the diaspora to gain their perspective and wisdom of life, love, and cultural knowledge. After these wonderfully divine experiences of enlightenment, I was confronted with a darkness I could not have ever imagined or hoped for myself or anyone.

In the blink of an eye, all the fears and nevers of my life begin to crash over me like giant waves, and as an African American who is apart of the 84 percent who cannot swim - I began to drown. These pivotal life choices and the experiences that came with them, allowed for me to break through the millennial illusion and begin to seek knowledge and truth within self-reflection and accountability. Thus came the creation of this book EMOETRY. It became a collection of prayers, thoughts, poems, and stories through the eyes of a woman who saw the despair, hope, and love in life from an emotional eye glass; all while pushing forward in society.

This book speaks from the wisdom within our spirit to the humanism that is within our heart. All the while, delicately balancing the wishes of lessons taught and the backlash of secrets kept. Many things that all women experience.

www.ingramcontent.com/pod-product-compliance
Lightning Source LLC
Chambersburg PA
CBHW062056280426
43673CB00085B/448/J